COOL SENSORY SUSPENSE

 Fun Science Projects about the Senses

Esther Beck

ABDO
Publishing Company

TO ADULT HELPERS

You're invited to assist an up-and-coming scientist! And it will pay off in many ways. Your children can develop new skills, gain confidence, and do some interesting projects while learning about science. What's more, it's going to be a lot of fun!

These projects are designed to let children work independently as much as possible. Encourage them to do whatever they are able to do on their own. Also encourage them to try the variations when supplied and to keep a science journal. Encourage children to think like real scientists.

Before getting started, set some ground rules about using the materials and ingredients. Most important, adult supervision is a must whenever a child uses the stove, chemicals, or dry ice.

So put on your lab coats and stand by. Let your young scientists take the lead. Watch and learn. Praise their efforts. Enjoy the scientific adventure!

VISIT US AT WWW.ABDOPUBLISHING.COM

Published by ABDO Publishing Company, 8000 West 78th Street, Edina, Minnesota 55439. Copyright © 2008 by Abdo Consulting Group, Inc. International copyrights reserved in all countries. No part of this book may be reproduced in any form without written permission from the publisher. The Checkerboard Library™ is a trademark and logo of ABDO Publishing Company.

Printed in the United States.

Design and Production: Mighty Media, Inc.
Art Direction: Kelly Doudna
Photo Credits: Kelly Doudna, iStockphoto/Maartje van Caspel, JupiterImages Corporation, Photodisc, Shutterstock
Series Editor: Pam Price
Consultant: Scott Devens

The following manufacturers/names appearing in this book are trademarks: Gedney, Helix, McCormick, Minute Maid, Play-Doh, Skippy

Library of Congress Cataloging-in-Publication Data
Beck, Esther.
  Cool sensory suspense : fun science projects about the senses / Esther Beck.
      p. cm. -- (Cool science)
  Includes index.
  ISBN 978-1-59928-910-6
  1. Senses and sensation--Experiments--Juvenile literature. 2. Science projects--Juvenile literature. 3. Science--Experiments--Juvenile literature. I. Title.

  QP434.B43 2007
  612.8--dc22
                                          2007014276

Contents

Science Is Cool

Welcome to the cool world of science! Before we get started, let's put on our thinking caps. What do the following things have in common?

- bubbles in soda pop
  - helium balloons that stay up in the air
    - sounds you hear through the headphones of your music player
    - a telescope that makes the faraway moon and stars appear closer
    - choosing your right or left eye to look through a camera viewfinder
- your ability to balance on one foot

Did you guess that what they have in common is science? That's right, science! When you think of science, maybe you picture someone in a laboratory wearing a long white coat. Perhaps you imagine a scientist hunched over bubbling beakers and test tubes. But science is so much more. Let's take another look.

Soda pop doesn't develop bubbles until you open the container. That's because of a science called chemistry. Chemistry also explains why helium inside a balloon causes it to rise through the air.

You listen to your favorite song through the headphones attached to your music player. You look at the moon and stars through a telescope. Both activities are possible because of a science called physics. Did you know that eyeglasses improve your vision for the same reason telescopes work?

You tend to use the same eye each time you look through a camera viewfinder. You might find it challenging to balance on one foot. The science of biology helps explain why. Did you know it's related to the reason most people use only their left hand or right hand to write?

Broadly defined, science is the study of everything around us. Scientists use experiments and research to figure out how things work and relate to each other. The cool thing about science is that anyone can do it. You don't have to be a scientist in a laboratory to do science. You can do experiments with everyday things!

The Cool Science series introduces you to the world of science. Each book in this series will guide you through several simple experiments and projects with a common theme. The experiments use easy-to-find materials. Step-by-step instructions and photographs help guide your work.

The Scientific Method

Scientists have a special way of working. It is called the scientific method. The scientific method is a series of steps that a scientist follows when trying to learn something. Following the steps makes it more likely that the information you discover will be reliable.

The scientific method is described on the next page. Follow all of the steps. These steps will help you learn the best information possible. And then you can draw an accurate conclusion about what happened. You will even write notes in your own science journal, just like real scientists do!

EVEN COOLER!

Check out sections like this one throughout the book. Here you'll find instructions for variations on the project. It might be a suggestion for a different way to do the project. Or it might be a similar project that uses slightly different materials. Either way, it will make your science project even cooler!

6

1. Observe

Simply pay attention to something. This is called observing. A good way to prepare for the next step is to make up a what, why, or how question about what you observe. For example, let's say you observe that when you open a bottle of soda pop and pour it into a glass, it gets bubbly. Your question could be, How do bubbles get into soda?

2. Hypothesize

Think of a statement that could explain what you have observed. This statement is called a hypothesis. You might remember that you also saw bubbles in your milk when you blew into it with a straw. So your hypothesis might be, I think somebody used a straw to blow into the soda before the bottle was sealed.

3. Test

Test your hypothesis. You do this by conducting an experiment. To test your hypothesis about how bubbles get into soda, you might mix up a recipe, blow into the liquid with a straw, quickly close the container, and then open it back up.

4. Conclude

Draw a conclusion. When you do this, you tie together everything that happened in the previous steps. You report whether the result of the experiment was what you hypothesized. Perhaps there were no bubbles in your soda pop recipe when you reopened the container. You would conclude that blowing through a straw is not how fizz gets into liquids.

Write It Down

A large part of what makes science science is observation. You should observe what happens as you work through an experiment. Scientists observe everything and write notes about it in journals. You can keep a science journal too. All you need is a notebook and a pencil.

THINK LIKE A SCIENTIST!
Look for a box like this one on the first page of each project. It will give you ideas about what to write in your science journal before, during, and after your experiments. There may be questions about the project. There may be a suggestion about how to look at the project in a different way. Your science journal is the place to keep track of everything!

At the beginning of each activity in this book, there is a section called "Think Like a Scientist." It contains suggestions about what to record in your science journal. You can predict what you think will happen. You can write down what did happen. And you can draw a conclusion, especially if what really happened is different from what you predicted.

As you do experiments, record things in your journal. You will be working just like a real scientist!

EVEN COOLER!
You can record more than just words in your journal. You can sketch pictures and make charts. If you have a camera, you can even add photos to your journal!

Safe Science

Good scientists practice safe science. Here are some important things to remember.

- Check with an adult before you begin any project. Sometimes you'll need an adult to buy materials or help you handle them for a while. For some projects, an adult will need to help you the whole time. The instructions will say when an adult should assist you.

- Ask for help if you're unsure about how to do something.

- If you or someone else is hurt, tell an adult immediately.

- Read the list of things you'll need. Gather everything before you begin working on a project.

- Don't taste, eat, or drink any of the materials or the results unless the directions say that you can.

- Use protective gear. Scientists wear safety goggles to protect their eyes. They wear gloves to protect their hands from chemicals and possible burns. They wear aprons or lab coats to protect their clothing.

- Clean up when you are finished. That includes putting away materials and washing containers, work surfaces, and your hands.

Cool Sensory Suspense

"Did you see that?" "Phew, what stinks?" "Ouch, that hurt!"

We often use phrases like these in response to **input** from our senses. So are you the **sensory** type? It turns out that we all are! Our senses, which are hearing, sight, smell, taste, and touch, are the ways we **perceive** the world around us.

When babies are born, their senses are already in working order. They can hear their mothers' voices and see their faces at close range. Babies can smell their moms, taste their milk, and feel their touch. The moment they enter the world, humans begin to gather information about their environments. And they rely on their senses the rest of their lives!

Some people aren't able to use all their senses. For example, blind people do not have sight. But the human body has a remarkable ability to make up for any sensory loss by relying more on other senses. People without sight often have highly developed senses of hearing and touch, for example. In general, everybody's senses are not the same. And as we age, some of our senses weaken.

Learning about the senses is fascinating. In fact, humans have been studying the senses since ancient times. Today scientists generally agree that human beings have more than five senses. However, scientists continue to study the five traditional senses. We still have a lot to learn about how the senses work with the brain to interpret information.

The activities in this book are a fun way for you to investigate the senses. Each activity gives detailed instructions about how to proceed. Be sure to keep detailed notes in your science journal. Then you can redo your experiments later and compare results.

Materials

You can probably find these supplies around the house.

paper

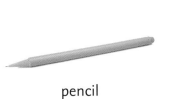
ruler

pencil

scissors

piece of paper with
a 7 mm (0.25 inch)
hole punched in it

cotton swabs

magnifying glass

paper cups

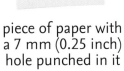
an empty can

pebbles or small rocks

coins

hairpins

gloves

a clock or a watch

12

AT THE GROCERY STORE
You can find these supplies at a grocery store.

orange juice

fruit punch

apple juice

food coloring

vinegar

orange peel

peanut butter

AT THE DISCOUNT STORE
You can find these supplies at a discount store.

blindfold

earplugs

small drum

modeling clay

nose plug

Which Is Your Dominant Eye?

MATERIALS

paper measuring
8.5 × 5.5 inches
(22 × 14 cm)

ruler

pencil

scissors

TIME: ABOUT 10 MINUTES

Use this simple test to see which
of your eyes you prefer to use.

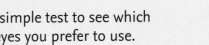

THINK LIKE A SCIENTIST!
Use both eye tests and compare
your findings. Then repeat
each test to **verify** your results.
Record all of the information in
your science journal.

14

1 Measure and draw a 1.25-inch (3 cm) square in the center of the paper.

2 Cut out the square. Using both hands, hold the paper in front of you at arm's length. Look at an object across the room.

3 Continue to focus on the object. Keep it centered in the hole and keep both eyes open. Now slowly bring the paper toward you until it's touching your face. The eye over which the cutout square is resting is your dominant eye.

The Science behind the Fun

Human beings have binocular vision. That means that our two eyes work together. But the dominant eye provides precise information about how objects are placed around us.

Here's how it works. The dominant eye looks directly at the objects it's viewing. The nondominant eye looks at the same object, but at a slight angle. This difference provides depth perception. So we are able to see how tall, wide, and deep an object is.

Science at Work

Scientists have found that about two-thirds of us are right-eye dominant. It's interesting to note that eye preference is not related to hand preference. Eye dominance is thought to be important in sports. This is especially true for sports that require excellent aim, such as archery.

Are You a Supertaster?

TIME: ABOUT 10 MINUTES

MATERIALS

piece of paper with a 7 mm (0.25 inch) hole punched in it

blue food coloring

cotton swabs

magnifying glass

a friend or a mirror

It's a bird. It's a plane. It's a supertaster? This quick investigation will show whether you're a person with super-strong taste powers.

BIOLOGY

THINK LIKE A SCIENTIST!

Make a list of your test subjects' names in your science journal. Record how many dots you counted on each person's tongue. Test as many people as you can. Then analyze the data. How do boys compare with girls? Do members of a family tend to have simlar numbers of dots? What other differences and similarities do you notice?

16

1 Place the paper with the hole on your tongue.

2 Using a cotton swab, "paint" over the hole with blue food coloring. Remove the paper. The circle on your tongue will be blue with white dots on it.

3 Have a friend count the dots in the blue circle. Or use a mirror to count your own dots!

4 Consult the table below to check your supertaster status.

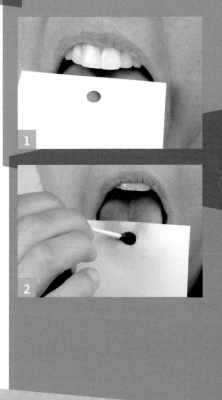

The Science behind the Fun

The small dots on your tongue are called **papillae**. These papillae house your taste buds. In this activity, your tongue soaks up the blue dye. But, the papillae stay white and are easy to count. Check the table to learn what your results mean.

Number of papillae	Means
15 or fewer	You're a nontaster.
between 15 and 35	You're an average taster.
more than 35	You're a supertaster!

Science at Work

Supertasters are more sensitive to bitter tastes than nontasters and average tasters are. Foods that supertasters tend not to enjoy include Brussels sprouts, cabbage, coffee, and grapefruit juice.

Sounds Important!

TIME: ABOUT 30 MINUTES

MATERIALS

noisemaking objects such as coins

an empty can

pebbles

a small drum

a blindfold

earplugs

BIOLOGY

Did you know that you need both ears to figure out where a sound is coming from? In this activity, you and a friend will work with earplugs, some noisemaking objects, and the space around you to investigate how your ears **perceive** sound.

THINK LIKE A SCIENTIST!
In your science journal, keep track of how the different listeners did. Then compare notes. Are some people better than others at identifying where sounds are coming from?

18

1 Gather a small group of friends. Choose one person to blindfold. This person should also place an earplug in one ear.

2 Have the other friends form a loose circle around the blindfolded person.

3 Silently choose a person in the circle to make a noise using an object you gathered for the activity. This person can rattle, click, tap, or clap, for example.

4 Have the blindfolded person try to identify where the sound is coming from. Be sure to record both who made the sound and the guess.

5 Now choose additional friends to make noises. Be sure to record each of the listener's guesses.

6 Remove the earplug. Repeat the noisemaking, again keeping track of the listener's guesses now that they're using both ears to hear.

7 Repeat the activity with different people in the listening role.

The Science behind the Fun

Sound localization is the ability to estimate where a sound is coming from. For human beings, sound localization requires both ears. Because our ears are on opposite sides of our heads, one ear usually receives a sound before the other. Our brains then use the information from both ears to determine where it is coming from.

When a sound is directly in front of us, it arrives in both ears at the same time. Then we don't need sound localization. That's why we often turn toward a sound when trying to hear where the sound is coming from.

Science at Work

Now that you know about sound localization, you'll probably want to go try it out. Just don't expect it to work underwater! That's because sound travels faster underwater than in air. Hearing underwater occurs by bone conduction. In other words, the skull bones transmit sounds to the inner ear.

Twin Taste Test

TIME: ABOUT 30 MINUTES

Have you ever plugged your nose when taking some bad-tasting medicine? Or have you "tasted" some delicious food before it ever hit your mouth? Then you probably already know that smell contributes to taste. Try this taste test on a group of friends to see just how closely the two senses are related.

MATERIALS

5 paper cups
orange juice
apple juice
fruit punch
water
food coloring
nose plug
one or more friends

BIOLOGY

THINK LIKE A SCIENTIST!

Data collection is an important part of this activity. Here's an example of a table you could use to collect your data. Or you can get creative and use your own method to track information. Just be sure to write it down. That's what all scientists do!

	Nose plugged	Nose unplugged
Drink 1		
Drink 2		
Drink 3		
Drink 4		
Drink 5		

1 Number five cups. Fill the cups with the drinks. There are four drinks and five cups, so two cups will have the same drink. Tricky! Be sure to write in your science journal which drink is in which cup.

2 Now add food coloring to each cup. Be sure to use the same color for each drink. Add as much as you need to so that all drinks look similar.

3 Have a friend plug her nose and drink from each cup, trying to guess which drink is in each one. Write down her guesses in your science journal.

4 After a short break, have your friend try the drinks again. But this time she should not plug her nose. Write down her guesses.

5 Compare your friend's guesses with the actual drink flavors. Was she able to identify the drinks correctly? Was she more accurate in one of the two rounds?

6 Repeat this taste test with as many people as you have supplies for. Keep track of all their guesses. What did you find?

Science at Work

Here's a classic example we've all experienced. When we have colds, we can't taste very well. That's because our noses are stuffed up and **out of commission**, which means everything pretty much tastes like chicken soup!

The Science behind the Fun

When we eat, it's not only our sense of taste that gives us flavor. It's also our sense of smell. When food is in our mouths, the taste buds on our tongues become active. And the smell of the food enters our noses through a connected passage. So the two senses work together. Makes sense!

What Does Your Nose Know?

TIME: ABOUT 15 MINUTES

MATERIALS
vinegar
pencil
orange peel
peanut butter
modeling clay
other scented items
friends and family members

Smells can trigger memories and emotions. In this activity, you'll close your eyes and smell an item to learn just what your nose really knows!

BIOLOGY

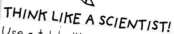

THINK LIKE A SCIENTIST!
Use a table like the one on page 24, or one of your own design, to keep track of your answers.

1 Have a friend close his eyes and smell one of the items you collected, such as the clay.

2 Ask him to rate the smell as weak, noticeable, or strong.

3 Then ask him, "What does it make you think of?" Write down his reply.

4 Next ask, "How does it make you feel?" Write down the answer.

5 And finally, ask if he can identify the smell. Write down the answer.

6 Repeat the above steps with the other items you collected, asking the same questions and recording the answers.

7 Compare different people's answers. Are the answers unique, or do the same smells **evoke** similar memories and emotions in your friends and family?

Draw a table like this one in your science journal to keep track of your data.

	Rate the smell. Is it weak, noticeable, or strong?	What does it make you think of?	How does it make you feel?	What do you think it is?
Item 1				
Item 2				
Item 3				
Item 4				
Item 5				

The Science behind the Fun

Information about smells travels from receptor cells in the nose to the part of the brain used for remembering events and feeling emotions. That's why smells can make people zero in on a particular memory. Smells can also make us feel happy, sad, or even anxious. Now that's a real sense of power!

Science at Work

Real estate agents often tell people to make their house fragrant when others come to see it. One way sellers do this is to bake cookies just before the house tour. The sweet smell of home-baked cookies will make buyers think of happy times in their past. And then they will have good feelings about the house. Just be sure the cookies don't burn!

Take a Sensitivity Test

TIME: ABOUT 15 MINUTES

MATERIALS

hairpins
friends

This activity will help determine how touch-sensitive different parts of the body are. All you really need are hairpins, test subjects, and some time!

	1 Hairpin Point	2 Hairpin Points
Back of Leg		
Elbow		
Inside of		
Palm		
Back		
Fingert		
Behind		
Lips		
Chin		

✏️ **THINK LIKE A SCIENTIST!**
This activity requires lots of data collection. Use your trusty science journal for the task. You'll want to draw a table like the one on page 26 for each person who takes the hairpin test.

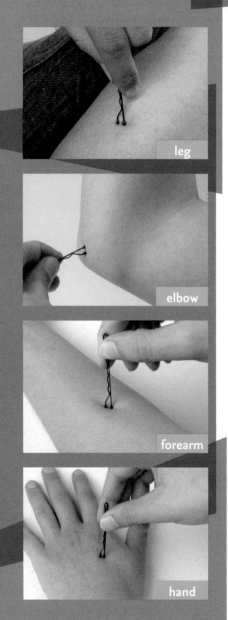

leg

elbow

forearm

hand

This science test is unique because the test subjects can test themselves! Be sure everyone takes care when placing the hairpins on their faces.

1 Give each test subject a hairpin and a table like the one shown below.

	Back of leg	Elbow	Inside of forearm	Palm	Back of hand	Fingertip	Behind neck	Lips	Chin
1 hairpin point									
2 hairpin points									

2 Have them shut their eyes while they safely touch the areas of their bodies noted in the table with the two points of the hairpin.

3 Test subjects should chart their own findings. For example, if they felt a single point on the elbow, put an X beneath "Elbow" in the "1 hairpin point" row. If they felt 2 points, place the mark in the "2 hairpin points" row.

4 Compare your results. What do you think it means when you feel two points? On which areas of the body did this occur?

EVEN COOLER!

Scientists put their data in graphs because it's an easier way to see patterns in the information. Use the data from all your test subjects to give this creative graph a try.

MATERIALS

large piece of paper   colored pencils

1. Draw an outline of a body on the paper.
2. Now it's time for you and your friends to add your data to this "body." Each person should place a yellow X on the part of the body where a single hairpin point was felt. Then place a green X on each part of the body where two points were felt.
3. How does this graph help you see which parts of the body are most sensitive to touch?

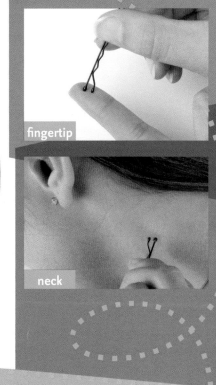

fingertip

neck

The Science behind the Fun

Human skin has nerve endings that make it sensitive to touch, pressure, and temperature. The nerves carry the information received by the nerve endings back to the brain. The number of nerve endings varies in different parts of the body.

Areas that have more nerve endings, such as our lips and fingers, are more sensitive to touch. When experimenting with the hairpins, sometimes people feel both points. Other times, the two points feel as if they are one. These findings help us know where there are more nerve endings.

Science at Work

Have you spent time around babies? They go through a stage when they'll put anything and everything in their mouths. That's because their lips have a lot of nerve endings and are excellent receptors. It's a baby's way of finding out about the world!

Subtracting Senses

TIME: ABOUT 90 MINUTES

MATERIALS

blindfold
(for sight)

earplugs
(for hearing)

nose plug
(for taste
and smell)

gloves
(for touch)

a clock or watch

a partner

BIOLOGY

Not all people are able to use all their senses. In this activity, you'll call on your powers of observation as you try operating minus a sense.

THINK LIKE A SCIENTIST!
Your science journal will come in handy during this activity. Be sure to take notes about your experience as you work through each step in the experiment. Compare notes with your partner. Were your experiences similar?

1 Choose one partner to go without one sense for 10 minutes. For example, blindfold your partner so he or she can experience being without the sense of sight. During this time, try to do everyday activities such as walking or eating.

2 After 10 minutes, take a break and write some notes about the experience. Both partners should contribute observations. What was most difficult about the experience? How did your partner help you?

3 Each partner should do both roles in this activity.

4 Now repeat the experiment, this time going without a different sense.

Science at Work

Some blind people use **echolocation** to help them navigate without sight. The technique involves sensing objects by hearing echoes off those objects. Some who use echolocation describe it as another sense rather than a learned technique!

The Science behind the Fun

While most people have the use of all senses, not all people do. The most obvious examples are blind people and deaf people. Head injuries can affect the senses of taste and smell as well. Loss of any sense makes life more difficult. But people who do not have a certain sense often develop ways of **compensating** for the loss. Sometimes they call on their other senses to do more.

Conclusion

If you enjoyed the activities in this book, continue your **sensory** investigations. Do you have a question about how your senses work? This question might be a good first step in developing your own activity.

You can ask your science teacher to help you think of a way to test your question. You'll also find many great experiments in the science section of your library. Science Web sites for students are another place to look.

Some of the experiments you find may be appropriate for your next school science fair. You'll be sure to impress the judges with all you know about the senses. And since you'll be investigating the human body, the activities are likely to involve other people and some fun!

Keep a list of the activities you want to try in your science journal. Then give them a whirl on the next rainy day. It will be sense-sational!

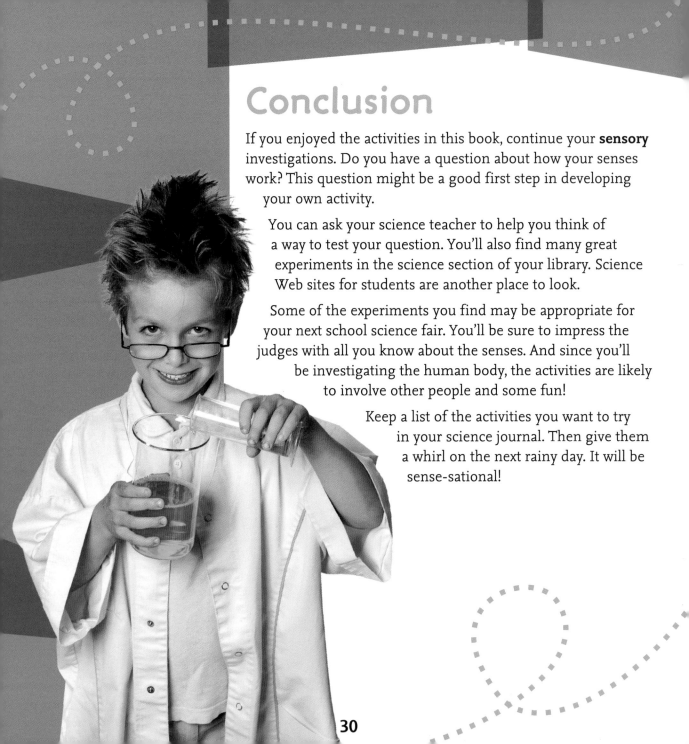

Glossary

compensate – to make up for an injury or a loss.

echolocation – a process for locating distant or unseen objects by using sound waves.

evoke – to call forth or bring something to mind.

input – information that is put into a project, process, or computer.

localization – confining or assigning to a particular area. *Sound localization* refers to the ability to determine the source of a sound.

out of commission – not in working order.

papilla – a bump on the surface of the tongue that contains taste buds. The plural of *papilla* is *papillae*.

perceive – to use senses such as sight or hearing to gather information about one's surroundings.

sensory – of or relating to the senses.

WEB SITES

To learn more about the senses and perception, visit ABDO Publishing Company on the World Wide Web at **www.abdopublishing.com.** Web sites about senses and perception are featured on our Book Links page. These links are routinely monitored and updated to provide the most current information available.

Index